AF269854

Christina Hammock Koch

C. KOCH
K. KУК

Christina Hammock Koch

Artemis Astronaut

Carla Mooney

LERNER PUBLICATIONS ◆ MINNEAPOLIS

Lerner Publications Company
An imprint of Lerner Publishing Group, Inc.
241 First Avenue North
Minneapolis, MN 55401 USA

For reading levels and more information, look up this title at www.lernerbooks.com.

Main body text set in Rotis Serif Std 55 Regular. Typeface provided by Adobe Systems.

Designer: Connie Kuhnz **Photo Editor:** Lucien Brinkley

Library of Congress Cataloging-in-Publication Data

Names: Mooney, Carla, 1970– author.
Title: Christina Hammock Koch : Artemis astronaut / Carla Mooney.
Description: Minneapolis : Lerner Publications, [2026] | Series: Gateway biographies
  | Includes bibliographical references and index. | Audience: Ages 9–14 | Audience:
  Grades 4–6 | Summary: "Readers discover the life story of NASA astronaut Christina
  Hammock Koch. Follow her incredible journey from humble beginnings in Grand
  Rapids, Michigan, all the way to the International Space Station and beyond"—
  Provided by publisher.
Identifiers: LCCN 2024060396 (print) | LCCN 2024060397 (ebook) | ISBN
  9798765669365 (lib. bdg.) | ISBN 9798765684115 (pbk.) | ISBN 9798765677490
  (epub)
Subjects: LCSH: Koch, Christina H., 1979-–Juvenile literature. | Women astronauts–
  United States–Biography–Juvenile literature. | Artemis Program (U.S.)–Juvenile
  literature. | Space flight to the moon–Juvenile literature. | Women engineers–United
  States–Biography–Juvenile literature.
Classification: LCC TL789.85.K59 M66 2026 (print) | LCC TL789.85.K59 (ebook) | DDC
  629.450092 [B]–dc23/eng/20250224

LC record available at https://lccn.loc.gov/2024060396
LC ebook record available at https://lccn.loc.gov/2024060397

Manufactured in the United States of America
1-1012012-53907-3/26/2025

TABLE OF CONTENTS

Christina Koch at NASA's Johnson Space Center in 2020

In the early morning of October 18, 2019, veteran NASA astronaut Stephanie Wilson spoke. Her calm voice echoed through the crew's radio headsets on the International Space Station (ISS). Wilson was on Earth at the Johnson Space Center in Houston, Texas. She was talking to astronauts Christina Koch and Jessica Meir. They were 250 miles (402 km) above Earth's surface in the ISS. Step by step, Wilson guided Koch and Meir through their final preparations for a space walk.

At 7:38 a.m., the hatch to the exterior airlock on the ISS opened. Koch emerged. She wore a bulky white space suit. Her first task was to ensure the safety tethers were in place. A safety tether is a critical piece of equipment for a space walk. It attaches an astronaut to the space station. It stops the astronaut from floating away into space. Koch made sure the safety tethers were in place. Then Meir slowly emerged from the airlock. She wore a nearly identical white space suit.

Koch and Meir had an important task. A battery

Koch replaces old batteries with new ones while tethered outside the ISS.

charge/discharge unit (BCDU) had failed outside the ISS a week earlier. The BCDU charged and discharged the solar-powered batteries that powered the space station's systems. Now, the astronauts needed to make an unplanned space walk to fix it.

Koch and Meir worked outside the ISS for hours. Wilson's voice guided them through their radio headsets. Fellow astronauts Luca Parmitano and Andrew Morgan supported the repair work from inside the ISS. The women successfully replaced the failed power charging unit.

At 2:55 p.m., Koch and Meir returned to the inside of the ISS. Their space walk lasted seven hours and seventeen minutes. It also made history. Koch and Meir were the first all-female space walk team. NASA streamed a live video of their space walk. People on Earth could watch the women work outside the ISS. Their white space suits glowed against the inky-black background of space as they made history.

It was Koch's fourth space walk. Meir was making her first. Koch appreciated each space walk she made. "The clarity of the Earth below you is absolutely stunningly beautiful. And how close it feels. Seeing nothing but a vibrant ocean beneath your feet is an amazing experience," she said.

On Earth, NASA astronaut Tracy Caldwell Dyson reflected on the history Koch and Meir had just made.

Sunset as seen from the ISS

"I think the milestone is hopefully this will now be considered normal . . . not to overshadow women [who] have been doing space walks for 35 years. I think many of us are looking forward to this just being normal," she said.

Early Years

Christina Hammock Koch was born in Grand Rapids, Michigan, on January 19, 1979. She spent much of her childhood in Jacksonville, North Carolina. Her father was a doctor. He was also an amateur astronomer. Her mother was a middle school math teacher. The Hammock home was always full of magazines about space and science. At the dinner table, Christina, her parents, and her three younger siblings would talk about the universe and other out-of-this-world subjects. Asking questions and learning new things were encouraged.

Christina loved the outdoors and wide-open spaces. She was an active child. She kept busy in sports such as swimming, running, and surfing. She learned how to sail with her father. Sailing on the ocean made her think about her place in the universe. She was fascinated with the exploration of distant lands. She cut out photos of Antarctica and other remote places from magazines. Then she taped them on her bedroom walls. "All of these places that were on the frontiers, places to be explored, just caught my interest from the time I was really young," she said.

Christina could look up from her backyard and see the

Christina's horizons expanded at the North Carolina School of Science and Mathematics.

stars shining in the night sky. It was there that she began to dream about going into space. She told people she would be an astronaut one day. She decorated her walls with posters of space shuttles.

Christina's parents encouraged her. They took her to visit the Kennedy Space Center in Florida. Christina was awed by the many exhibits about space exploration. It made her even more determined to explore space someday.

Christina worked hard in school, especially in STEM (science, technology, engineering, and math) subjects. She joined her middle school's rocket club. In high school, she was accepted to the North Carolina School of Science and Mathematics. It was a prestigious school. At first, Christina was intimidated by her classmates, but she learned an important lesson. "This was the first time I got a taste of something that I've tried to hold onto: using intimidation or feeling scared to actually fuel your success, to turn it around and use that as motivation to achieve what you might not have thought was possible before," she said.

Christina attends NASA's Space Camp as a teen.

In 1992 Christina attended NASA's Space Camp in Huntsville, Alabama. There, she learned about the space program. She trained like an astronaut and participated in simulated missions. "Space Camp was a place where I found out I wasn't the only one dreaming to be a part of the space program. I met lifelong friends and people from all over the country," she said. She loved it so much she went every summer from 1992 to 1996.

Koch attended North Carolina State University after high school. She studied electrical engineering and physics. "I didn't want to just make things and not understand the theory behind it," she said. "And I didn't want to just have theory without being able to use my hands and create things." Koch excelled at North Carolina State and earned a 4.0 GPA. She got her bachelor's degree in electrical engineering in 2001. After that, she earned a bachelor's degree in physics in 2002.

Koch also completed the NASA Academy program in 2001. The NASA Academy is a ten-week summer research program. It's for college and graduate students interested in careers in space. In the program, Koch participated in a team research project. She learned about the space program and explored NASA research facilities.

Koch stayed at North Carolina State for graduate school. She earned a master's degree in electrical engineering in 2002. Her studies sharpened her engineering and technology skills.

What It Takes to Be a NASA Astronaut

Becoming an astronaut is a lofty goal. Very few people are chosen to live out their dreams in space. There are several requirements for NASA astronauts. First they must be US citizens. There are no official age restrictions, but most candidates are twenty-six to forty-six years old. Candidates must have strong math, science, and technology skills. They must have a master's degree in engineering, physics, or a related STEM field. Being physically fit is also essential. Space travel is hard on the body. Candidates must pass a physical exam to be sure they can handle the stress. NASA now also requires candidates to have logged one thousand hours of flight training. Some applicants meet this requirement in the military. Others fly commercial or private aircraft.

Electrical Engineer

Koch wanted to work in jobs that challenged her after college. She also wanted to explore the world. "I definitely like the idea of exploring, going somewhere new, and places where there are physical challenges along with the intellectual challenges," she said.

From 2002 to 2004, Koch worked as an electrical engineer at the Goddard Space Flight Center (GSFC) in Greenbelt, Maryland. She was in the Laboratory for High Energy Astrophysics. Astrophysics is a branch of space science that uses physics and chemistry to understand the larger universe. It explores stars, planets, galaxies, and other space objects.

The position allowed Koch to participate in the space program. She helped develop science instruments for the ISS. She gained valuable experience in different areas of space and technology.

Exploring Antarctica

Koch loved her engineering job at NASA. But in 2004, she stunned her coworkers by announcing she was leaving NASA. She had taken a job as a research associate for the United States Antarctic Program. Antarctica is one of the harshest environments on Earth. Koch knew the choice was a big change. But she firmly believed it was the right next step for her. "I knew I was passionate about exploring and science on the frontiers, and I knew that

Christina Koch at the South Pole in 2006

meant I had to go to Antarctica," she said.

Koch helped scientists conduct research in Antarctica for over three years. As part of her research, Koch spent a year at the South Pole. It's the coldest place on Earth. "I will never forget the first moment I stepped off the military aircraft that brought us all down to the South Pole. I basically just did a 360, looking around in all directions. I couldn't believe I had landed somewhere so remote, so foreign to everything I had ever known, and was actually there. Then I realized I couldn't feel my hands, and it was very cold," she said. While Koch was at Antarctica's Amundsen-Scott South Pole Station, temperatures dropped to –111°F (–79°C). Winds can be extreme, and 98 percent of the land there is covered in ice.

Koch stands beside a tank of liquid helium. Liquid helium is used to keep important parts of telescopes cold.

Keeping the scientists and support personnel safe is a top concern in Antarctica. But sometimes unexpected events happen. Every station has a search and rescue team. The team is trained in first aid, wilderness survival, and other essential skills. Koch joined the station's firefighting and search and rescue teams while at the South Pole. She trained weekly with the teams. They had to keep their survival skills sharp. They prepared in case they were needed to rescue someone in trouble.

Living in Antarctica was challenging both mentally and physically. The South Pole experiences the "polar night" from late April until mid-September. During the winter, the sun disappears. There is twenty-four-hour darkness for months. This causes extreme cold and sea ice. It makes traveling unsafe for airplanes or ships. "[It] means going months without seeing the sun, with the same crew, and without shipments of mail or fresh food. The isolation, absence of family and friends, and lack of new sensory inputs are all conditions that you must find a strategy to thrive within," Koch said about her experience.

Koch found ways to handle the difficult environment.

She regularly exercised. She socialized with others living at the station. She also saved care packages from family and friends to open later. "The most helpful strategy I developed was to avoid thinking about all the things I was missing out on and instead focused on the unique things in the moment that I would never get to experience again," she said.

One of those unique things was Antarctica's southern lights. Auroras put on a brilliant natural light show in the sky throughout the winter. Shimmering ribbons of green, red, and violet swirled in the sky. Koch had never lived somewhere she could see auroras. "I fell in love with this phenomenon, the southern lights," she said. She dreamed about one day seeing the auroras from space.

Researchers at the South Pole must adapt to the twenty-four-hour darkness that lasts for months in this part of the world.

Beautiful Auroras

Auroras are lights in the night sky. They are often seen near the North and South Poles. They are caused by particles, which are called ions, from the sun that travel through space. They mix with gases such as oxygen and nitrogen when they hit Earth's atmosphere. The energy released by the collisions makes the gases glow. This creates beautiful lights in the sky. Earth's magnetic field directs the sun's particles toward the North and South Poles. That is why auroras are most often seen there. The northern lights are most easily seen in Alaska, Canada, and Norway. The southern lights appear near the South Pole.

In Antarctica, Koch gained valuable experience working in extreme environments. She showed that she could still pursue science, engineering, and fieldwork in one of the most extreme environments on Earth. It gave her the skills she would need as an astronaut. And it helped prepare her for the demands of spaceflight.

Supporting Science in Space

Koch returned to the United States in 2007. She began work as an electrical engineer in the Applied Physics Laboratory at Johns Hopkins University. She dove back into developing science instruments for space. Koch helped develop the Jupiter Energetic Particle Detector Instrument (JEDI). The JEDI was designed and built for a NASA mission to Jupiter called the Juno mission. Its goal was to gather data to better understand Jupiter. The JEDI was an essential part of this mission.

NASA opened applications for a new group of astronauts in 2009. Koch was tempted to apply. But she decided to pass on the chance. She wanted to finish her work on the JEDI. In 2011 Koch watched the Juno mission launch into space carrying the JEDI. "It was great to see something to fruition," she said.

Outside the lab, Koch was an active rock climber. She practiced lead climbing, a style of climbing where the climber has no rope above them to catch them if they fall. Lead climbers must learn how to protect themselves

from falling. "It taught me something really important. You can rely on yourself to get out of situations when they are quite frankly scary, and with enough focus and enough confidence, you can actually overcome obstacles," Koch said.

In 2010 Koch returned to remote scientific work. She spent time at Palmer Station in Antarctica. She worked several winter seasons at Greenland's Summit Station. In Greenland she saw the northern lights. In 2012 Koch took a position with the National Oceanic and Atmospheric Administration (NOAA). She was headed to Barrow, Alaska.

While in Alaska, Koch heard about another NASA call for astronauts. This time, she applied. "What actually inspired me to make the move to actually do the application was just reflecting on my career and realizing that through following my own personal dreams, I had accumulated a set of skills that I thought could really be useful in contributing to human space flight," she said. Over six thousand people applied. Koch hit Send on her application. Then she returned to her work.

Koch had moved on to her next position. She was station chief for NOAA on the small island of American Samoa when she got a call from NASA. They wanted to interview her for the astronaut program. Koch flew from the South Pacific to Houston for a week of interviews. "Interestingly, the one thing the [NASA] interview committee wanted to talk to me the most about wasn't electrical engineering, it was about rock climbing, and working in Antarctica, and all these other experiences that I had that were part of my path to get there," Koch said about the NASA interviews.

About a week after her interviews, Koch received a call from NASA. They had chosen her as one of eight candidates in NASA's twenty-first astronaut class. Koch's dreams of going to space were about to come true.

Becoming an Astronaut

Koch had to keep her astronaut news a secret for two weeks. NASA asked her to tell only one person until they made the official announcement. Koch chose her boyfriend, Robert Koch. "The one person I told was my boyfriend at the time, who is now my husband! I'll never forget the look on his face when I broke the news. I've never seen him look so happy or surprised since," she said.

In June 2013, NASA announced the twenty-first astronaut class. Koch was part of an eight-member class of four men and four women. Each brought different backgrounds and experiences to the space program.

Sally Ride

Years before Koch made history at the ISS, another female astronaut was breaking barriers. In 1983 Sally Ride (*above*) became the first American woman to travel to space. Born in 1951, Ride loved science and math as a child. She went on to earn a master's degree in physics. In 1977 NASA placed a newspaper ad for scientists to join the space program. Ride answered the ad. She was one of five women chosen for NASA's astronaut class of 1978. In 1983 Ride was one of five astronauts on the space shuttle Challenger STS-7. She launched two communication satellites during the mission and helped operate the shuttle's robotic arm. She also conducted several important experiments in space. Ride returned to space on the Challenger in 1984. She became a role model for women and girls interested in science and space exploration. Ride passed away in 2012, but her legacy still inspires future space explorers.

The candidates began an intense training program at the Johnson Space Center near Houston, Texas.

They studied a lot of topics, which included basic sciences and technology, mathematics, geology, meteorology, oceanography, astronomy, engineering, and physics. Outside the classroom, Koch trained in land and sea survival skills as well as scuba diving. Like all astronaut candidates, Koch was required to pass a swimming test. She had to swim three lengths of a 25-meter (82-foot) pool and tread water for ten minutes while wearing a flight suit and sneakers.

Koch soared through flight training. She learned how to fly high-performance aircraft. All astronauts must learn how to pilot aircraft to prepare for spaceflight. "It took every bit of grit and dedication to get through that course. Along with the challenge of learning skills like this is the everyday challenge of adapting to the wide range of new circumstances you encounter in this job," Koch said.

Koch also spent time on a plane nicknamed the vomit comet. The NASA plane simulated microgravity conditions for training astronauts. It

A modified KC-135A is used in the Reduced-Gravity Program to train and test humans and hardware in a low-gravity environment.

Johnson Space Center

The Lyndon B. Johnson Space Center is in Houston, Texas. It is NASA's main training facility for astronauts. The massive campus has unique training rooms and detailed simulators. Scientists help astronauts train and prepare for missions. And it is the

An aerial view of the Johnson Space Center facility

home of mission control. From there, scientists and engineers guide astronauts while they are in space. The Johnson Space Center opened in 1961 and has acted as home base for many of NASA's projects. It was the base for NASA's Space Shuttle program from 1981 to 2011. And these days it's the main hub of NASA's research and development efforts. It is also the headquarters for several current space programs. These include ISS missions and the Artemis program.

got its nickname because it caused many people to get sick.

In addition, Koch spent hundreds of hours learning to use the ISS computer systems and spacecraft on lifelike simulators. Simulators re-create the environment astronauts will experience in space, and they model the computer systems astronauts use in space. Koch practiced operating the ISS's robotic arm. She also studied Russian. She wanted to be able to speak to the Russian astronauts on the ISS. Two of the first words she learned in Russian

US astronauts Christina Koch (*left*) and Nick Hauge (*right*) alongside Russian cosmonaut Alexey Ovchinin in 2019

were *tired* and *busy*. They are words astronauts often use when discussing their experience in space! One of Koch's favorite parts of training was preparing for space walks. Koch practiced at the bottom of a gigantic indoor pool at the Neutral Buoyancy Laboratory. "You get to wear a full space suit just like the ones they use in orbit. Working with a big team, we go through the entire choreography of a flight-like space walk while underwater in a giant pool that has a full mockup of the outside of the International Space Station!" Koch said. "It is very physically demanding as well, so I loved the challenge of having to get super in-shape just to be ready to focus on learning the tools and skills needed for the space walk tasks."

Koch graduated from the astronaut training program in 2015. However, her preparations for space were just beginning. She would spend four more years training before her first spaceflight.

The launch of the Soyuz MS-12 spacecraft in 2019. Koch, Hague, and Ovchinin were aboard.

On the ISS

It took six years of training, but Koch was finally ready for space. On March 14, 2019, she boarded the Soyuz spacecraft in Kazakhstan in central Asia. Koch launched with NASA astronaut Nick Hague and Russian cosmonaut Alexey Ovchinin. They traveled for six hours until they docked at the ISS.

The International Space Station

The ISS (*below*) is a large spaceship that orbits over 250 miles (400 km) above Earth. It is a giant laboratory in space where astronauts live and work. It measures 356 feet (109 m) long, almost the size of a football field. It orbits Earth about sixteen times a day.

Astronauts do cutting-edge science experiments on the ISS. They study such things as plants, animals, and the human body while in space. The ISS helps scientists learn more about space, Earth, and how people can live in space. It also helps research and test technologies used in space and back on Earth.

The ISS is a symbol of international cooperation. It was designed and built by scientists and astronauts from the United States, Russia, Japan, Canada, and other countries. Its components were built worldwide. Then they were launched and put together in space. The ISS is the largest human-built object to ever orbit Earth. Astronauts have lived on the ISS since November 2000. More than 260 people from twenty-one countries have visited the ISS.

Koch was the first to enter the ISS. She greeted the crew, which consisted of NASA astronaut Anne McClain, Canadian astronaut David Saint-Jacques, and Commander Oleg Kononenko from Russia. Standing inside the ISS for the first time was a dream come true for Koch. "That was the day that I have seared in my memory. Visions from when I first arrived here . . . I'm very privileged to have that as one of my favorite memories," she said.

Over the next eleven months, Koch conducted and supported more than two hundred scientific investigations aboard the ISS. Her research was vast. It ranged from biology and Earth science to technology development. She helped test free-flying robots inside the space station. The crew investigated Earth's atmospheric carbon cycle. Koch tested a three-dimensional bioprinter. This was to try printing organ-like tissues in microgravity. She also helped improve the station's Alpha Magnetic Spectrometer. It collects data from galaxies millions of light-years away from Earth.

Koch also volunteered to be a research subject while in space. Scientists could study the effects of a long-duration spaceflight on a woman. One investigation studied how spaceflight affected bones and muscles in the spine. The research will be important as NASA plans future missions to the moon and Mars. It will help scientists develop ways to reduce damage for future astronauts.

Koch completed six space walks at the ISS. One of those was the first all-female space walk with NASA astronaut Jessica Mier. She spent a total of forty-two hours and fifteen minutes on space walks. Her first space walk was on

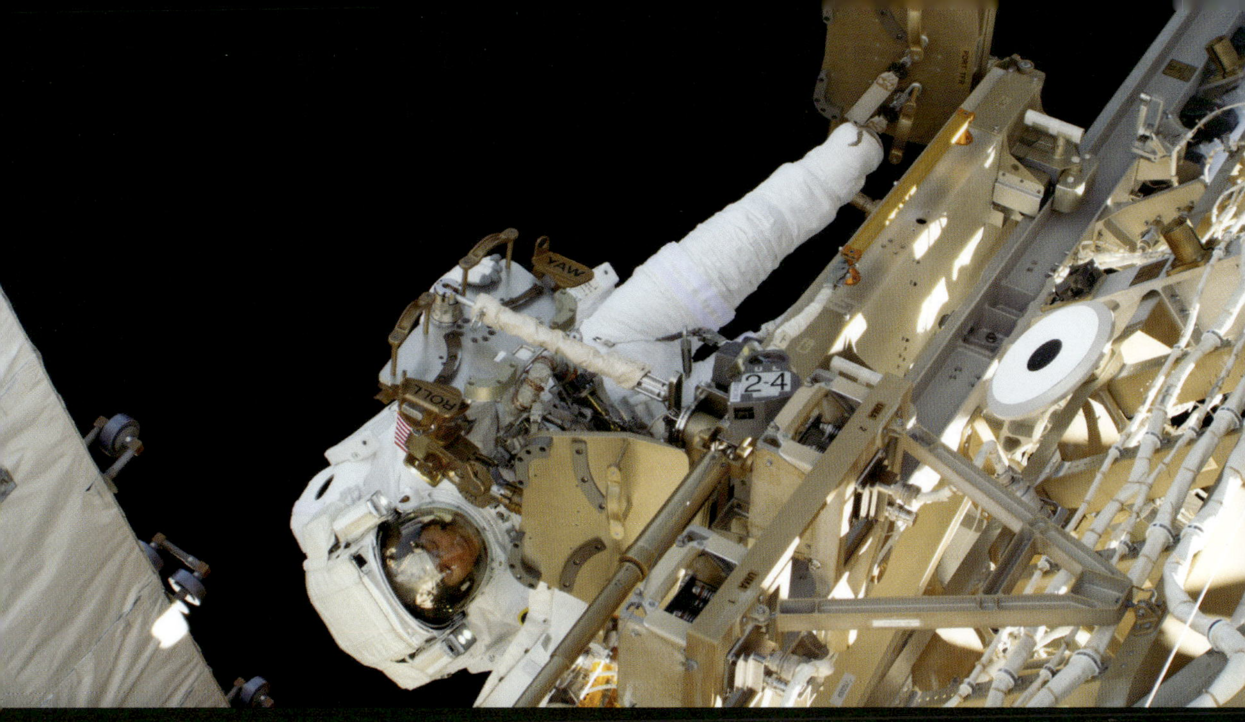

Koch takes her first space walk outside the ISS.

March 29, 2019. She marveled at how clearly she could see Earth outside the station. "At that moment, I just felt like everything I had ever worked for, everything I had ever loved, everything I had ever wanted to contribute to my entire life was just culminating in that moment," she said.

When Koch went to sleep, she stayed in a sleeping bag in a tiny room. The room was about the size of a phone booth. The sleeping bag was attached to the wall or ceiling. This was to keep her from floating around. Koch worked with resistance machines to reduce the loss of muscle and bone density from low gravity. She even had some time for fun. The crew sang karaoke and held pizza nights. They played pickleball with a blob of floating water. And she treasured the handwritten letters from her husband. They arrived with cargo supply vehicles.

Koch left the ISS on February 6, 2020. She landed back on Earth in Kazakhstan. Koch had been in space for 328 days. And she had set a record. It was the longest single spaceflight in history for a woman. Koch orbited Earth 5,248 times and traveled 139 million miles (224 million km) during her mission.

As she exited the spacecraft back on Earth, Koch smiled broadly and gave a thumbs-up. Then she headed to her postflight medical checkups. She was looking forward to things she missed while in space. She wanted to feel the sensations of wind and rain, sand under her feet, and the sound of the ocean near her home in Galveston, Texas.

Hours later, Koch posted a message about her experience on social media: "This journey has been everyone's journey. Thank you to all involved in the success of our mission and for giving me the opportunity to carry everyone's dreams into space. I'm filled with gratitude to be back on the planet!"

Back to the Moon

In 1969 astronauts Neil Armstrong and Buzz Aldrin landed on the moon. They were part of NASA's Apollo program. Fifty years later, NASA announced a new program. They wanted to send astronauts back to the moon. The program was named Artemis after the Greek goddess of the moon. The program planned to land on

Astronaut Buzz Aldrin walks on the surface of the moon in 1969. A leg of the Lunar Module is visible on the right.

the moon's south pole, somewhere no human has ever set foot. NASA will use new technology on the Artemis missions to study the moon and to prepare for future missions to Mars.

The Artemis program planned to use NASA's new powerful rocket. It was called the Space Launch System (SLS). It would carry the Orion spacecraft into orbit around the moon. The Orion can carry up to four astronauts. It will dock in space at a small spaceship called the Gateway. From there, the astronauts will travel to the moon's surface. Then they will return to the Gateway. After completing their work, the astronauts will come back to Earth on the Orion.

Several Artemis missions were needed to test the rocket, spacecraft, and systems before landing astronauts on the moon. The first Artemis test mission, Artemis I, launched in November 2022. It completed a crewless test flight of the SLS rocket and the Orion spacecraft.

The SLS rocket carries the Orion spacecraft as it launches in 2022.

The next step was to test the SLS and Orion with an astronaut crew. In April 2023, NASA and the Canadian Space Agency announced the four-person crew of Artemis II. It would be the first crewed mission to orbit the moon in nearly fifty years. Artemis II will fly around the moon before returning to Earth. It will be the farthest any human has traveled in space. The agencies chose four experienced astronauts: Reid Wiseman, Victor Glover, Christina Hammock Koch, and Jeremy Hansen. Koch was thrilled to be going back to space. "It means a great deal to me to be involved in any way that I can in truly answering humanity's call to explore," she said.

The Artemis II mission was scheduled to launch in September 2025. Koch and other astronauts began to prepare. It was an intense training program. They spent hundreds of hours learning inside a simulator of the Orion capsule at the Johnson Space Center in Texas. The cone-shaped space capsule is tight quarters for four people. It measures about 12 feet (3.6 m) across and less than 5 feet (1.5 m) tall in most places. Moving through the capsule with three other people involves crouching and ducking. "It's a lot bigger in 3D, when you can float around," Koch said. "That's what I'm telling myself."

Training in the simulator is critical. The astronauts learn the systems and the layout of the Orion spacecraft. They practice rocket burns and docking maneuvers needed to orbit Earth. The astronauts also train for different scenarios. Unexpected problems occur in these trainings. The problems give the astronauts practice for handling problems in space.

The Orion spacecraft moves away from Earth and approaches the moon on the first day of the Artemis I mission.

"Their training is preparing them to do everything from planned mission tasks and daily operations to how to recognize and deal with unexpected situations," said Jacki Mahaffey, chief training officer for Artemis II.

The astronauts also trained in the Pacific Ocean. They practiced how they will get out of the capsule once it lands back on Earth. They traveled to Iceland to learn more about volcanic geology. It is similar to what they will see on the moon's surface. In September

Space walk training is often done underwater to simulate low-gravity environments.

2023, Koch and Hansen traveled to the Mistastin crater in Newfoundland, Canada, for more geology training. They practiced identification, taking samples, and photographing geological features.

If everything goes according to schedule, Koch will return to space in 2025. Although Artemis II will not land on the moon, it is a critical step toward that goal. "Our primary task is observing, observing the moon. Our job is to tell the scientists back home the things that lunar probes can't see or tell. And that is, what colors do human eyes see? What observations, large scale, do we see? And we're being trained to do just that, to describe and observe. It's a supreme responsibility to have eyes on the far side of the moon," she said.

The Future of Science and Space

In 2023 Koch and her Artemis II crew visited Capitol Hill in Washington, DC. They had a series of meetings with members of Congress. As the astronauts posed for a few photos, a group of tourists passed them. Koch heard one of the tourists exclaim excitedly, "Did you see that? One of them was a woman!" The moment reminded Koch of the importance of her role. She was inspiring future scientists and space lovers.

Talking about her achievements as a woman in science and space was not always easy for Koch. She loved

Left to right: Artemis II crew members Reid Wiseman, Victor Glover, Christina Koch, and Jeremy Hansen

The Artemis II crew attends a White House staff briefing in 2024.

mentoring others and sharing her experiences. But she was also humble. She felt uncomfortable highlighting everything she had achieved. "I originally shirked away from the idea of talking about a record or number of days or those things. But I was actually taught by people that I talked to about it that milestones mean something to people. And sharing them helps educate where we are, the state of the art of human exploration. Inspiration for people that might be up against things that are challenging for them," she said.

Koch has remained passionate about volunteering, tutoring, and encouraging a love of science in others. Her inspiration for the younger generation shows at her former high school in Jacksonville, North Carolina. On the wall outside a science classroom, students in the school's science club painted a mural in Koch's honor. The mural includes one of Koch's quotes: "Follow your

Koch's official 2018 NASA portrait

passions, live the life you've imagined and do what scares you." Across from the mural, a glass case is filled with Koch's yearbook photos and mementos.

Koch has received numerous awards for her work in space and on Earth. This includes the 2020–2021 Neil Armstrong Award of Excellence. The Astronaut Scholarship Foundation (ASF) grants the award to a scholarship alumnus every year. While studying at North Carolina State University, Koch received the ASF scholarship in 2000 and 2001. "Christina is a true inspiration to all Astronaut Scholars, as well as the next generation. We are tremendously proud, not only of her achievements in breaking new ground for women in STEM, but also for demonstrating that dreams can become a reality through commitment and persistence," said Curt Brown, chair of ASF's board of directors.

Koch has dreamed of space since she was five, staring at the stars in her backyard. She knows how lucky she is to be in a job she loves. Koch is happy to have the opportunity to inspire others. "I think, overall, flying in space is the dream job," she said. "You get to be in a place where you have this amazing perspective on Earth; you get to, you know, carry everyone's dreams with you in space; hopefully inspire people, and then your day-to-day is doing science and maintenance. And I can't imagine a better job than that."

IMPORTANT DATES

1979   Christina Hammock Koch is born on January 19 in Grand Rapids, Michigan.

2001   Koch graduates from North Carolina State University with a bachelor's degree in electrical engineering.

2002   Koch graduates from North Carolina State University with a bachelor's degree in physics and a master's degree in electrical engineering.

Koch begins work as an electrical engineer at the Goddard Space Flight Center, developing science instruments for space.

2004   Koch announces that she has joined the US Antarctic Program.

2007   Koch takes an engineering job with the Applied Physics Laboratory. She develops instruments for NASA's Juno mission to Jupiter.

2010   Koch returns to remote scientific work in Antarctica and Greenland's Summit Station.

2012   Koch joins the National Oceanic and Atmospheric Administration (NOAA) in Barrow, Alaska. She later becomes NOAA's station chief in American Samoa.

2013	NASA selects Koch as one of eight astronaut candidates. She moves to Houston where she begins astronaut training at Johnson Space Center.
2015	Koch graduates from astronaut candidate training to become an astronaut. She begins training for a mission to the International Space Station.
2018	NASA selects Koch as one of eighteen astronauts for the Artemis program, which will send crews to the moon.
2019	Koch launches to the ISS on March 14. On October 18, she completes the first all-female space walk with NASA astronaut Jessica Meir.
2020	Koch returns to Earth on February 6. She spent a record-breaking 328 days in space, the longest for a woman.
2023	Koch is selected as one of four astronauts for the Artemis II mission. She begins training at the Johnson Space Center.
2025	Koch is scheduled to return to space with Artemis II. The mission will fly the Orion spacecraft around the moon and return to Earth. The trip will be the farthest spaceflight for any human.

SOURCE NOTES

9 Ashley Strickland, "After an Historic All-Female Spacewalk, Astronaut Has Moon Dream," CNN.com, October 21, 2019, http://www.cnn.com/2019/10/21/world/nasa-all-female-spacewalk-reflections-scn-trnd/index.html

10 Chelsea Gohd, "NASA Astronauts Make History with 1st All-Woman Spacewalk," Space.com, October 18, 2019. https://www.space.com/first-all-woman-spacewalk-nasa-success.html.

10 Bill Krueger, "The Right Stuff," *NC State Magazine*, January 15, 2016, https://magazine.ncsu.edu/2016/the-right-stuff/.

11 "Astronaut Christina Hammock Koch '97 Followed Her Own Path to Space," North Carolina School of Science and Mathematics, March 8, 2016, https://www.ncssm.edu/news/astronaut-christina-hammock-koch-97-followed-her-own-path-to-space.

12 Lee Roop, "Artemis II: 5-Time Space Camp Alum Christina Koch Among NASA Astronauts Tapped for Moon Mission," Al, April 3, 2023, https://www.al.com/news/2023/04/artemis-ii-5-time-space-camp-alum-christina-koch-among-nasa-astronauts-tapped-for-moon-mission.html.

12 Krueger, "The Right Stuff."

14 Krueger.

14–15 Steven Devadanam, "The New Women of NASA," *Houstonia*, May 31, 2016, https://www.houstoniamag.com/new-and-city-life/2016/05/nasa-women-astronauts-mars-june-2016.

15 Jon Evans, host, *1on1 with Jon Evans*, podcast, "Christina Koch: Her Lifelong Dream of Going to Space Began Along the NC Coast," WECT, May 22, 2020, https://www.wect.com/2020/05/22

christina-koch-her-lifelong-dream-going-space-began-along-nc
-coast-with-jon-evans-podcast/.

16 "Antarctica Provides ICE to Study Behavior Effects in Astronauts,"
    Labxchange.org, modified April 12, 2024, https://www.labxchange
    .org/library/items/lb:LabXchange:41815b52:html:1.

17 "Antarctica Provides ICE to Study Behavior Effects in
    Astronauts."

17 "Astronaut Christina Hammock Koch '97 Followed Her Own Path
    to Space."

19 "Astronaut Christina Hammock Koch '97 Followed Her Own Path
    to Space."

20 "Astronaut Christina Hammock Koch '97 Followed Her Own Path
    to Space."

20 Danielle Herman, "N.C. State Grad Joins Space Race," *Business
    North Carolina*, July 30, 2018, https://businessnc.com/n-c-state
    -grad-joins-space-race/.

21 "Astronaut Christina Hammock Koch '97 Followed Her Own Path
    to Space."

21 Kristen Bobst, "Interview with Astronaut Christina Koch," *Teen
    Vogue*, September 27, 2017, https://www.teenvogue.com/story
    /interview-with-astronaut-christina-koch.

23 Bobst.

25 Bobst.

28 Jennifer Hernandez, "Christina Koch Shares Most Memorable
    Moments in Space," Roundup Reads, January 31, 2020, https://
    roundupreads.jsc.nasa.gov/roundup/1349.

29 Hernandez.

30 Nick Natario, "NASA Astronaut's Husband Excited for Wife's
    Return to Galveston," ABC13 Houston, February 7, 2020, https://
    abc13.com/christina-koch-nasa-astronaut-space-flight-female
    -record/5909289/.

33 Shelly Brisbin, "Astronaut Christina Koch Is 'Answering Humanity's
    Call to Explore,'" KUT Radio, April 21, 2023, https://www.kut
    .org/texasstandard/2023-04-21/nasa-astronaut-christina-koch
    -artemis-ii-moon-mission.

33 Scott Detrow et al., "Meet the Astronauts Preparing to Travel
    Farther from Earth Than Any Human Before," NPR, September
    28, 2024, https://www.npr.org/2024/09/27/nx-s1-5100867/nasa
    -moon-space-artemis-2-mission.

34 Rachel Kraft, "First Artemis Crew Trains for Mission Around
    Moon," NASA, October 19, 2023, https://www.nasa.gov/general
    /first-artemis-crew-trains-for-mission-around-moon/.

35 Detrow et al., "Meet the Astronauts."

36 Macarena Vidal Liy, "Christina Koch: 'When I Told My
    Kindergarten Teachers I Wanted to Be an Astronaut, They
    Supported Me,'" EL PAÍS English, May 20, 2023, https://english
    .elpais.com/science-tech/2023-05-20/christina-koch-when-i-told
    -my-kindergarten-teachers-i-wanted-to-be-an-astronaut-they
    -supported-me.html.

37, 39 Liy.

39 Deja Mayfield, "Teacher, Coach of Christina Koch, Speaks About
    Her Former Student's Space Exploration," WCTI, April 4, 2023,
    https://wcti12.com/news/local/teacher-coach-of-christina-koch
    -speaks-about-her-former-students-space-exploration.

39 "Astronaut Scholarship Foundation Honors Christina H. Koch with the 2020–2021 Neil Armstrong Award of Excellence," SpaceNews, March 9, 2021, https://spacenews.com/astronaut -scholarship-foundation-honors-christina-h-koch-with-the-2020 -2021-neil-armstrongac-award-of-excellence/.

39 Amy Thompson, "NASA Astronaut Christina Koch Is Breaking Records and Inspiring the Next Generation," Space.com, December 15, 2021, https://www.space.com/nasa-astronaut -christina-inspire-kids-stem-iss-research.

SELECTED BIBLIOGRAPHY

"Antarctica Provides ICE to Study Behavior Effects in Astronauts."
Labxchange.org. Modified April 12, 2024. https://www.labxchange
.org/library/items/lb:LabXchange:41815b52:html:1.

"Astronaut Christina Hammock Koch '97 Followed Her Own Path to
Space." North Carolina School of Science and Mathematics, March 8,
2016. https://www.ncssm.edu/news/astronaut-christina-hammock
-koch-97-followed-her-own-path-to-space.

Detrow, Scott, Ashley Brown, and Michael Levitt. "Meet the Astronauts
Preparing to Travel Farther from Earth Than Any Human Before."
NPR, September 28, 2024. https://www.npr.org/2024/09/27/nx-s1
-5100867/nasa-moon-space-artemis-2-mission.

Devadanam, Steven. "The New Women of NASA." *Houstonia,* May 31,
2016. https://www.houstoniamag.com/news-and-city-life/2016/05
/nasa-women-astronauts-mars-june-2016.

Gohd, Chelsea. "NASA Astronauts Make History with 1st All-Woman
Spacewalk." Space.com, October 18, 2019. https://www.space.com
/first-all-woman-spacewalk-nasa-success.html.

Hernandez, Jennifer. "Christina Koch Shares Most Memorable Moments
in Space." Roundup Reads, January 31, 2020. https://roundupreads
.jsc.nasa.gov/roundup/1349.

Kraft, Rachel. "First Artemis Crew Trains for Mission Around Moon."
NASA, October 19, 2023. https://www.nasa.gov/general/first-artemis
-crew-trains-for-mission-around-moon/.

Krueger, Bill. "The Right Stuff." *NC State Magazine,* January 15, 2016.
https://magazine.ncsu.edu/2016/the-right-stuff/.

Liy, Macarena Vidal. "Christina Koch: 'When I Told My Kindergarten
Teachers I Wanted to Be an Astronaut, They Supported Me.'" EL PAÍS
English. May 20, 2023. https://english.elpais.com/science-tech
/2023-05-20/christina-koch-when-i-told-my-kindergarten-teachers
-i-wanted-to-be-an-astronaut-they-supported-me.html.

Strickland, Ashley. "After an Historic All-Female Spacewalk, Astronaut
Has Moon Dream." CNN.com. October 21, 2019. http://www.cnn
.com/2019/10/21/world/nasa-all-female-spacewalk-reflections-scn
-trnd/index.html

LEARN MORE

International Space Station
https://www.nasa.gov/international-space-station/

NASA Astronaut Christina Koch
https://www.nasa.gov/people/christina-koch/

Rector, Rebecca Kraft. *The International Space Station.* Children's Press,
2022.

Rose, Rachel. *Christina Koch: Astronaut and Engineer.* Bearport, 2021.

Shepherd, Crown. *Changemakers in Space: Women Leading the Way.*
Lerner Publications, 2024.

US Antarctic Program
https://www.usap.gov

INDEX

PHOTO ACKNOWLEDGMENTS

Image credits: NASA/Beth Weissinger, p. 2; NASA/Bill Ingalls, pp. 6, 26, 36, 37; NASA/JSC, pp. 8, 22, 24, 29, 31, 34, 35; NASA, pp. 9, 27; Ildar Sagdejev/Wikimedia Commons (CC BY-SA 3.0), p. 11; U.S. Space & Rocket Center, Home of Space Camp®, p. 12; Thomas Fuller/SOPA Images/LightRocket via Getty Images, p. 13; Christina Hammock/National Science Foundation (CC BY-NC-ND 4.0.), pp. 15, 16; Tenedos/Getty Images, p. 17; Cavan Images/Per-Andre Hoffmann/Getty Images, p. 18; Christina Hammock/JHUAPL, p. 20; NASA/MSFC, p. 23; Pool Photo via AP, p. 25; NASA/Joel Kowsky, p. 32; NASA/Bill Stafford, p. 38.

Cover: NASA/Josh Valcarcel.